NUMBER TRACING BOOK

FOR PRESCHOOLERS

Zero

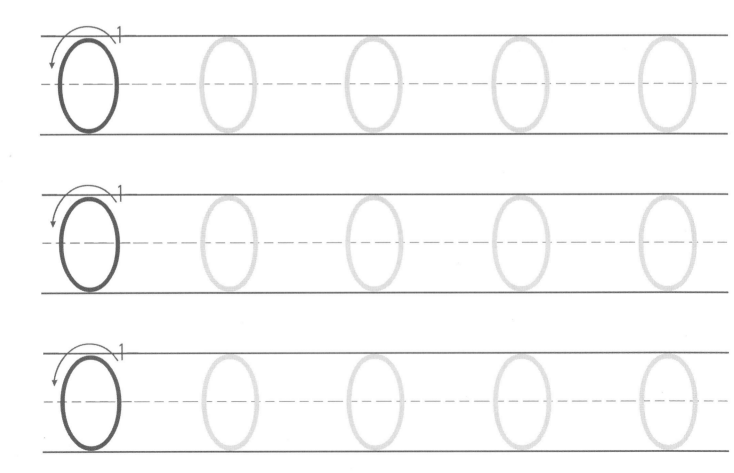

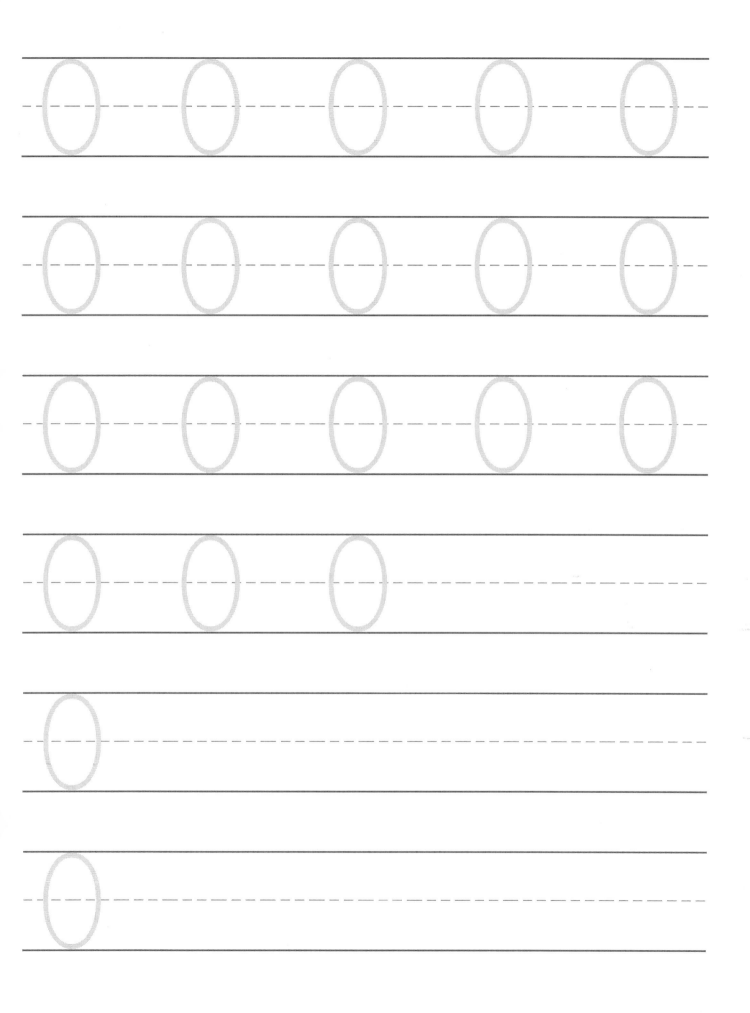

One

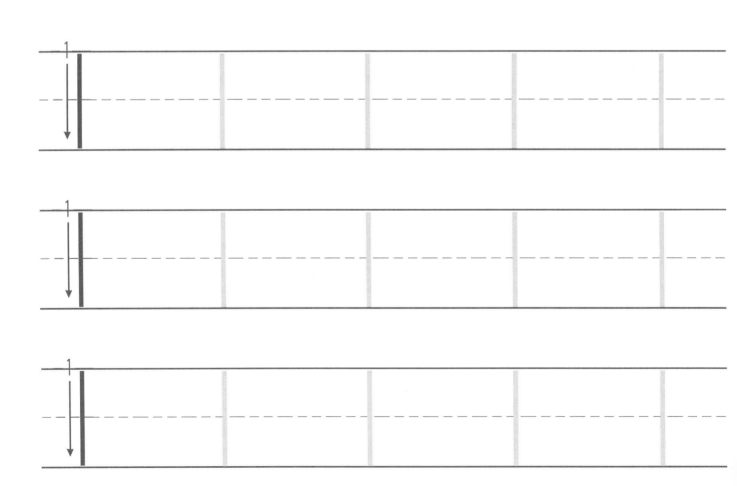

Two

2

2 2 2 2 2

2 2 2 2 2

2 2 2 2 2

2 2 2 2 2

2 2 2 2 2

2 2 2 2 2

2 2 2

2

2

Three

3

3   3   3   3   3

3   3   3   3   3

3   3   3   3   3

3　3　3　3　3

3　3　3　3　3

3　3　3　3　3

3　3　3

3

3

Four

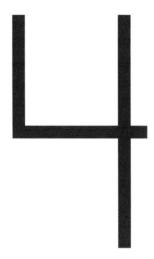

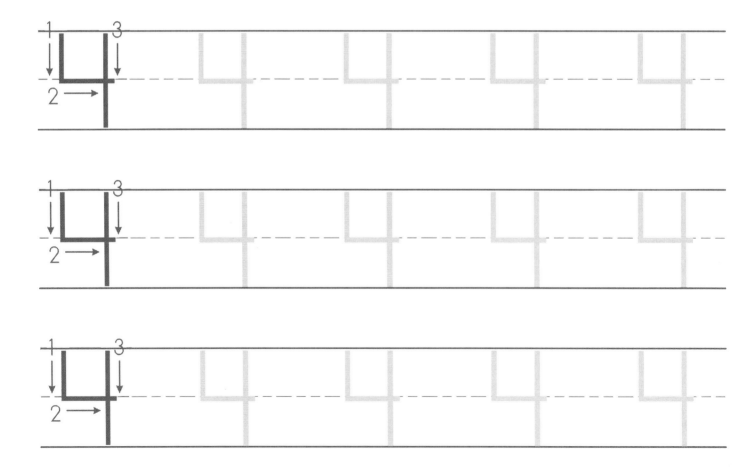

Five

5

5　5　5　5　5

5　5　5　5　5

5　5　5　5　5

5　5　5

5

5

Six

6

6　6　6　6　6

6　6　6　6　6

6　6　6　6　6

6 6 6 6 6

6 6 6 6 6

6 6 6 6 6

6 6 6

6

6

Seven

7

1 → 2
7 7 7 7 7 7

1 → 2
7 7 7 7 7 7

1 → 2
7 7 7 7 7 7

Eight

8

8
8 8 8 8

8
8 8 8 8

8
8 8 8 8

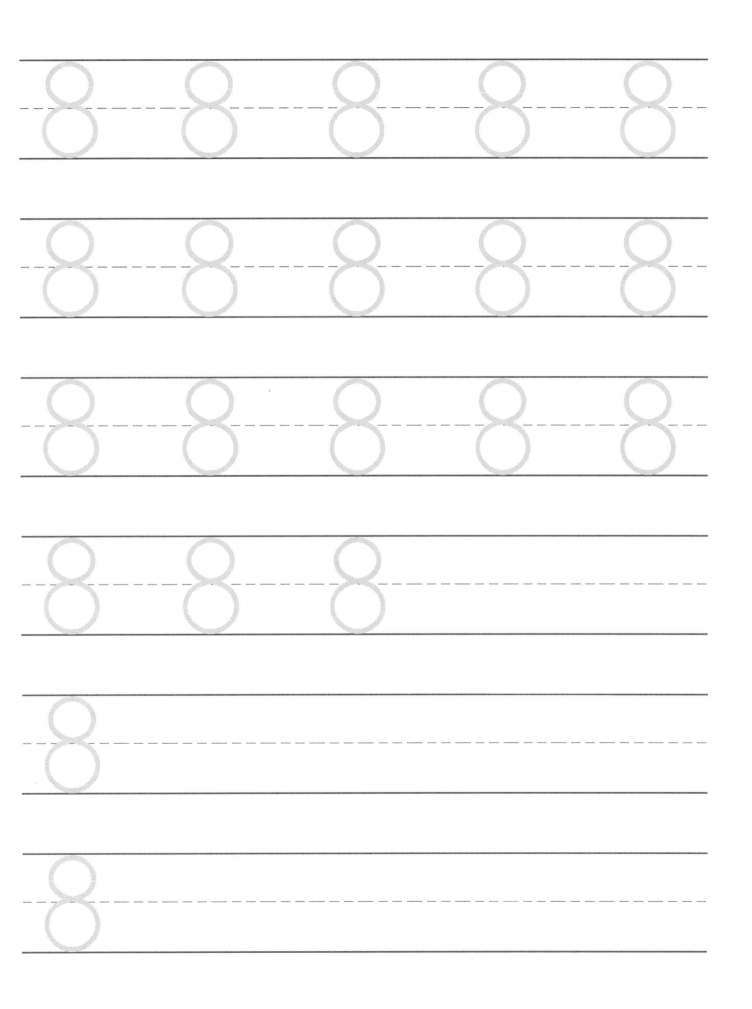

Nine

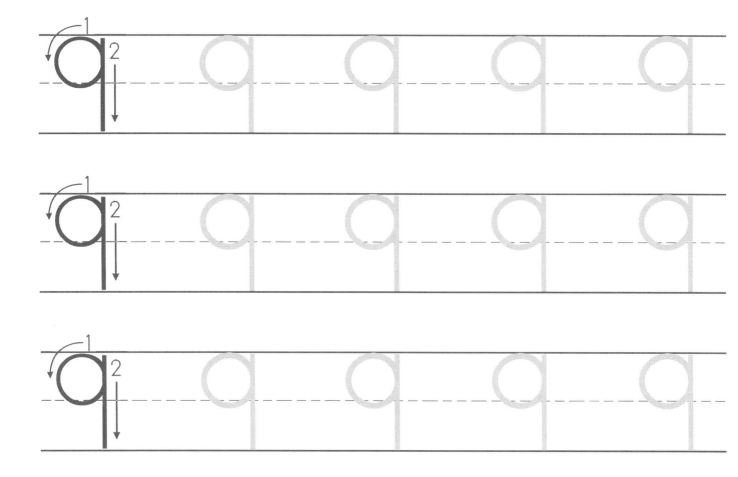

Ten

10

10 10 10 10

10 10 10 10

10 10 10 10

10   10   10   10

10   10   10   10

10   10   10   10

10   10

10

10

Tracing the numbers.

Tracing the numbers.

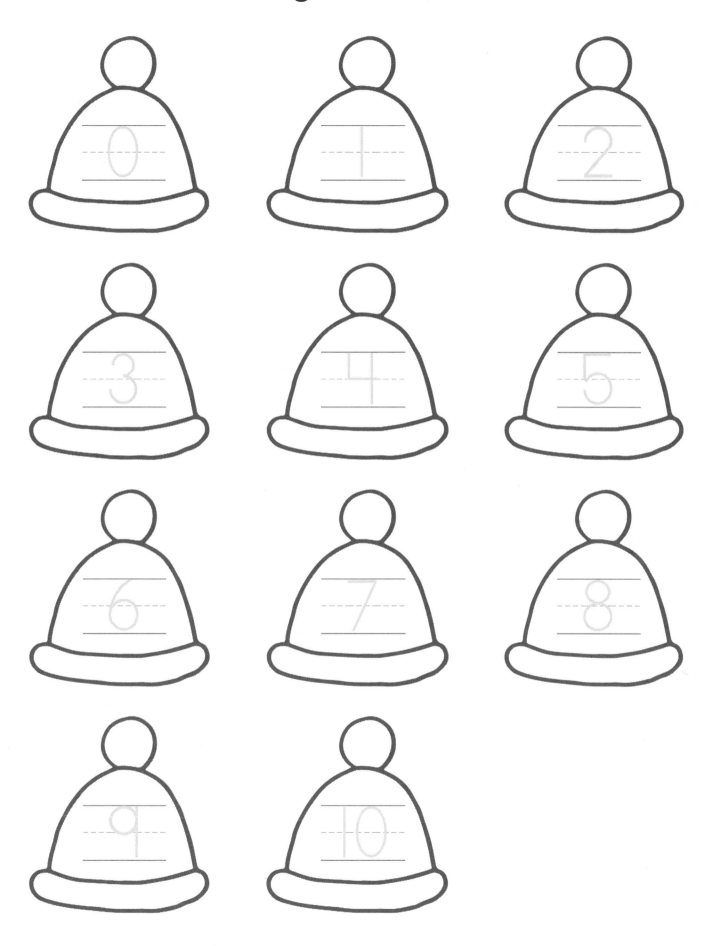

Tracing the numbers.

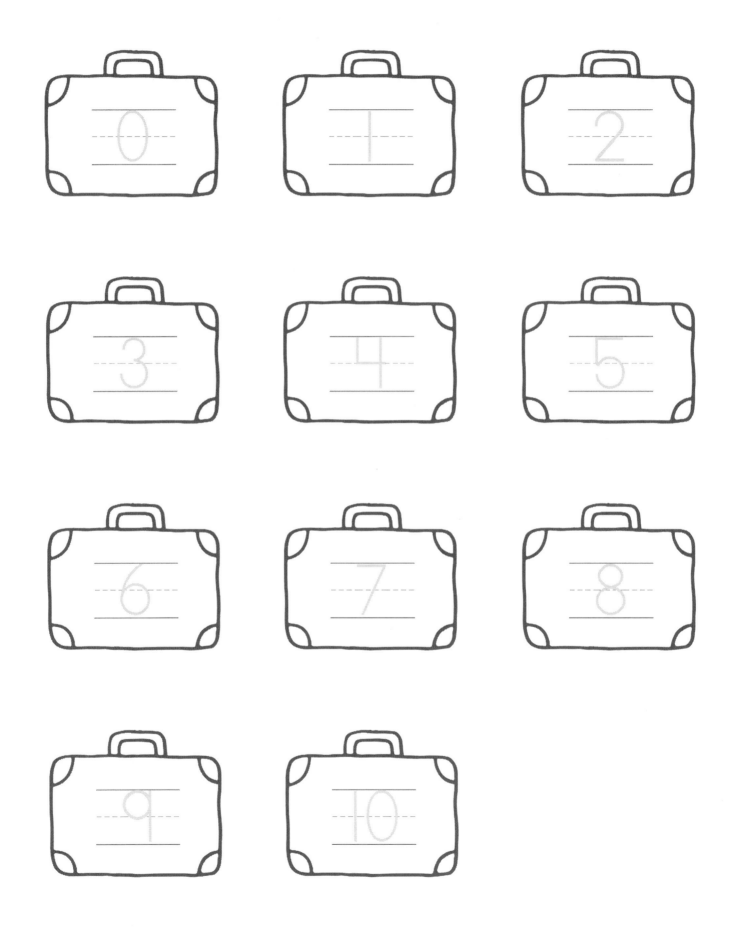

Tracing the numbers.

Tracing Line Practice

Trace each line matching number and number word.

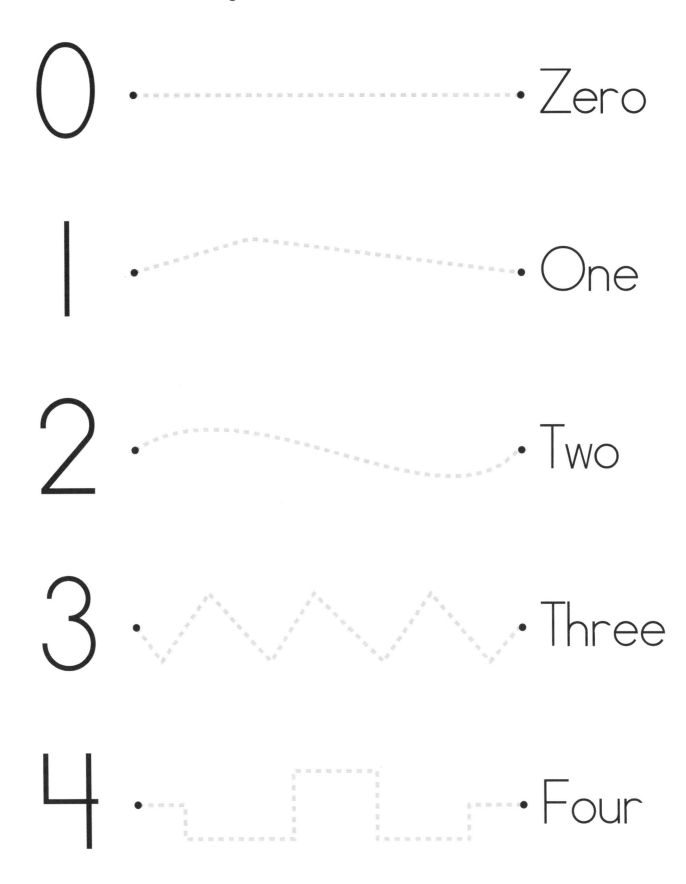

5 • Five

6 • Six

7 • Seven

8 • Eight

9 • Nine

10 • Ten

Tracing Line Practice

Trace each line matching number and number word.

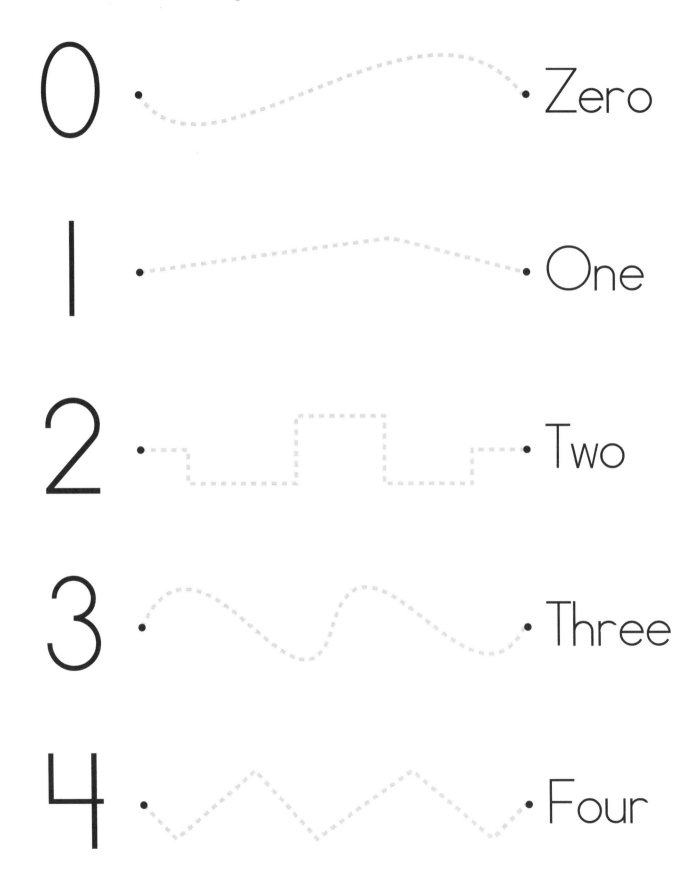

5 •·······•· Five

6 •·······• Six

7 •·······• Seven

8 •·······• Eight

9 •·······• Nine

10 •·······• Ten

Tracing Line Practice

Trace each line matching number and number word.

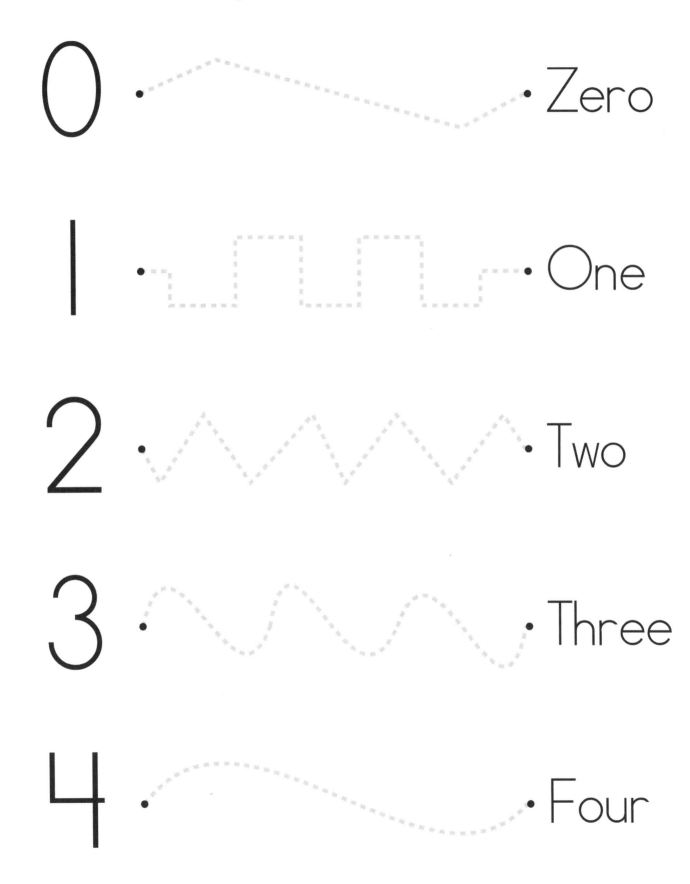

5 • · • Five

6 • · • Six

7 • · • Seven

8 • · • Eight

9 • · • Nine

10 • · • Ten

Tracing Line Practice

Trace each line matching number and picture.

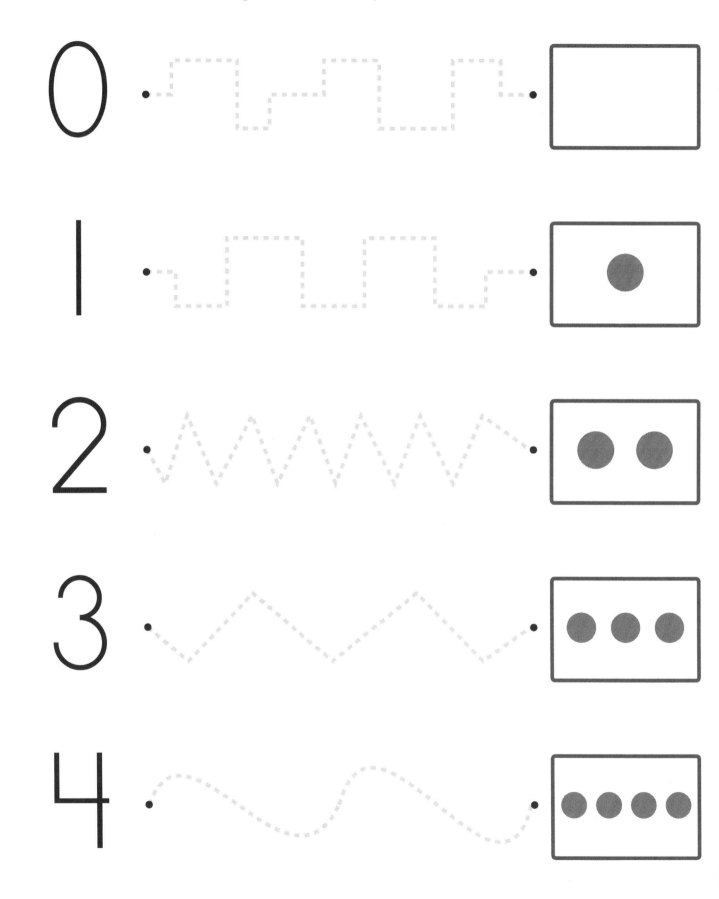

5

6

7

8

9

10

Tracing Line Practice

Trace each line matching number and picture.

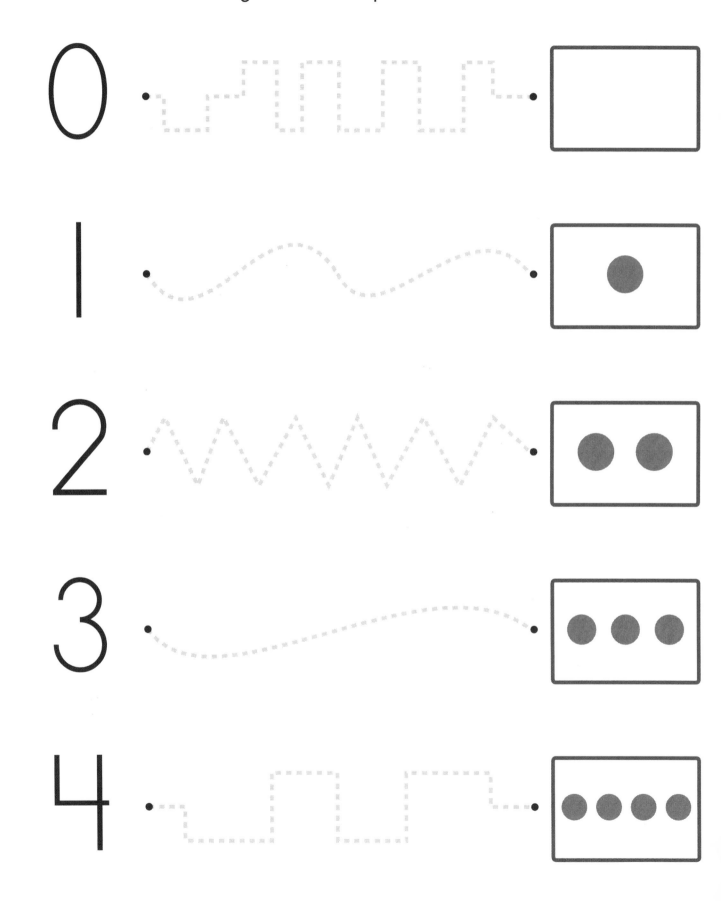

5

6

7

8

9

10

Eleven

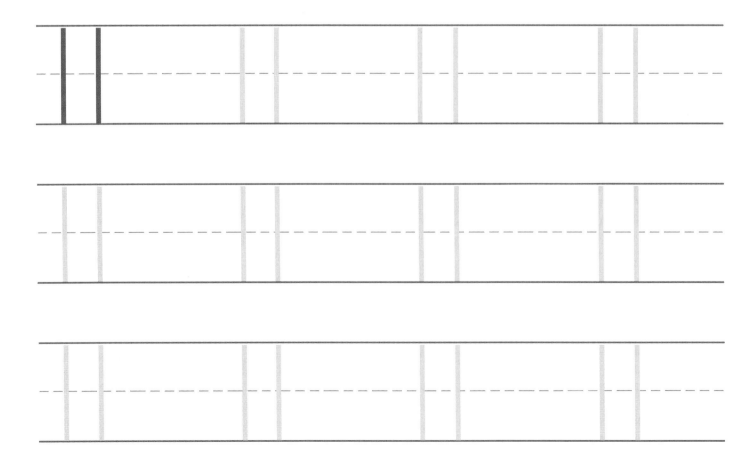

Twelve

12

12 12 12 12

12 12 12 12

12 12 12 12

12 12 12 12

12 12 12 12

12 12 12 12

12 12

12

12

Thirteen

13

13　13　13　13

13　13　13　13

13　13　13　13

3 3 3 3

3 3 3 3

3 3 3 3

3 3

3

3

Fourteen

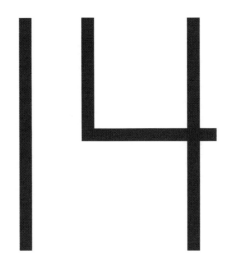

Fifteen

15

15　15　15　15

15　15　15　15

15　15　15　15

15   15   15   15

15   15   15   15

15   15   15   15

15   15

15

15

Sixteen

16

16 16 16 16

16 16 16 16

16 16 16 16

16   16   16   16

16   16   16   16

16   16   16   16

16   16

16

16

Seventeen

17

17 17 17 17 17 17

17 17 17 17 17 17

17 17 17 17 17 17

17 17 17 17

17 17 17 17

17 17 17 17

17 17

17

17

Eighteen

18

18 18 18 18

18 18 18 18

18 18 18 18

8 8 8 8

8 8 8 8

8 8 8 8

8 8

8

8

Nineteen

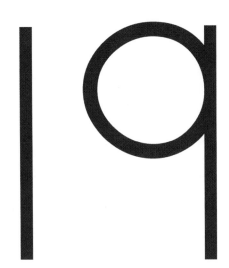

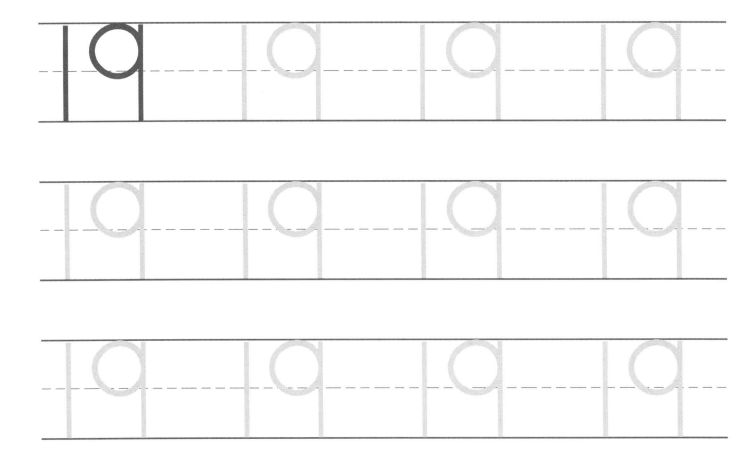

a a a a

a a a a

a a a a

a a

a

Twenty

20

20 20 20 20 20

20 20 20 20 20

20 20 20 20 20

20 20 20 20 20

20 20 20 20 20

20 20 20 20 20

20 20

20

20

Tracing the numbers.

Tracing the numbers.

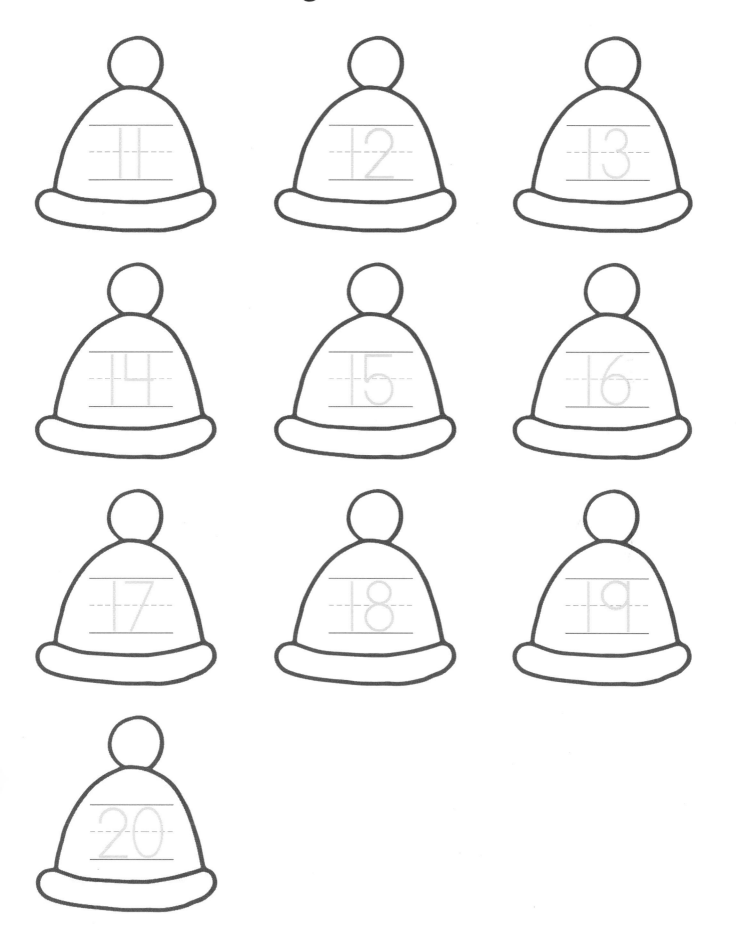

Tracing the numbers.

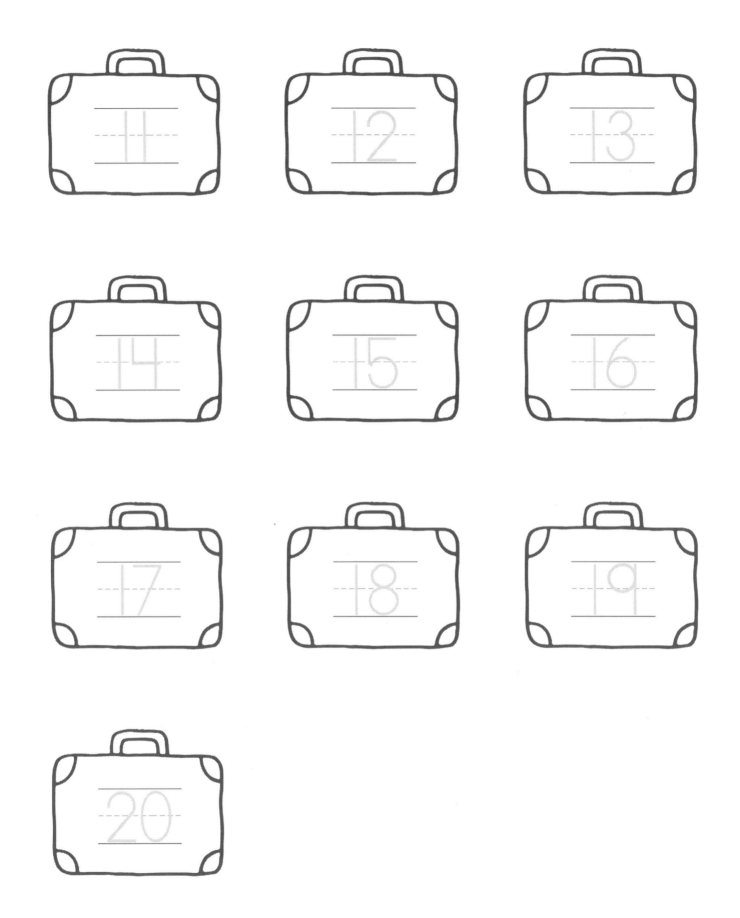

Tracing the numbers.

Tracing Line Practice

Trace each line matching number and number word.

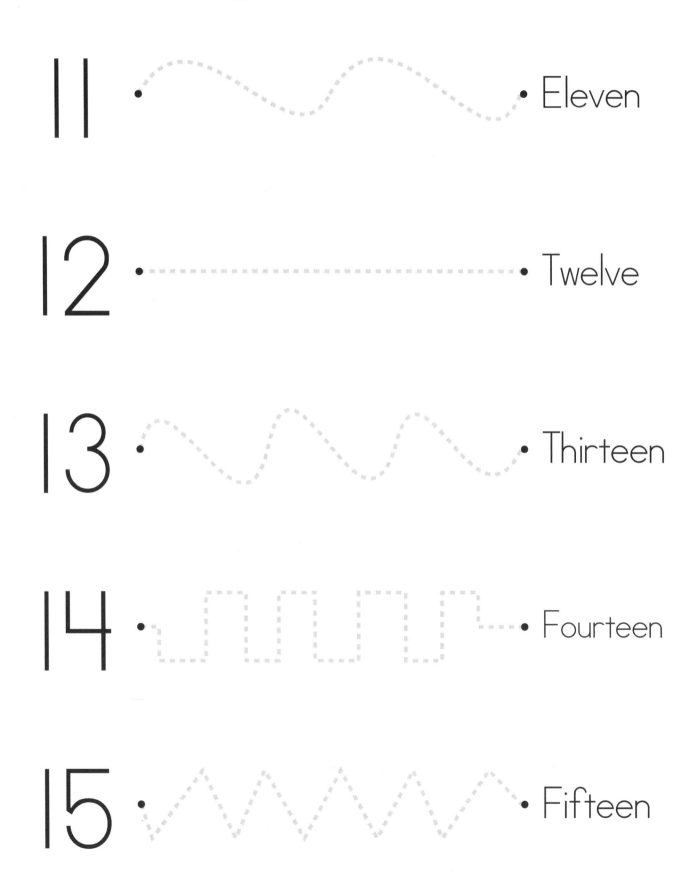

11 • ⋯ • Eleven

12 • ⋯ • Twelve

13 • ⋯ • Thirteen

14 • ⋯ • Fourteen

15 • ⋯ • Fifteen

16 • - - - - - - - • Sixteen

17 • - - - - - - - • Seventeen

18 • - - - - - - - • Eighteen

19 • - - - - - - - • Nineteen

20 • - - - - - - - • Twenty

Tracing Line Practice

Trace each line matching number and number word.

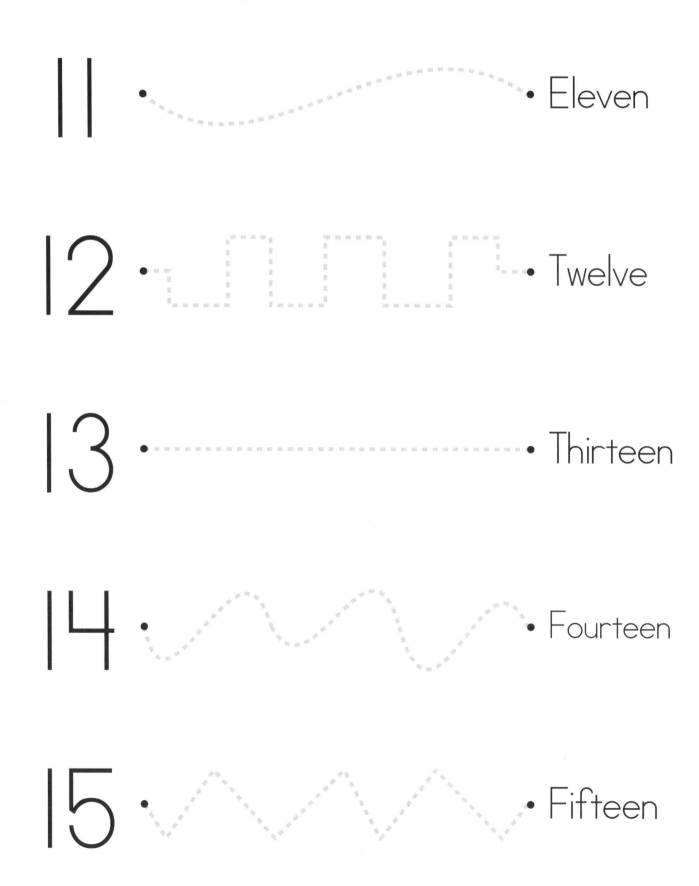

11 • • Eleven

12 • • Twelve

13 • • Thirteen

14 • • Fourteen

15 • • Fifteen

16 •·····• Sixteen

17 •·····• Seventeen

18 •·····• Eighteen

19 •·····• Nineteen

20 •·····• Twenty

Tracing Line Practice

Trace each line matching number and number word.

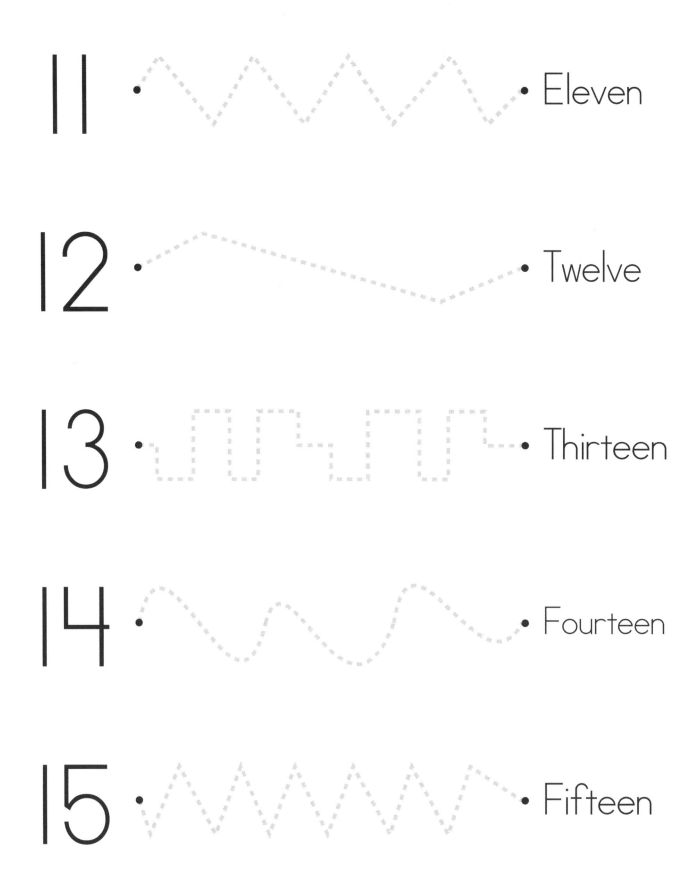

11   Eleven

12   Twelve

13   Thirteen

14   Fourteen

15   Fifteen

16 • • Sixteen

17 • • Seventeen

18 • • Eighteen

19 • • Nineteen

20 • • Twenty

Tracing Line Practice

Trace each line matching number and picture.

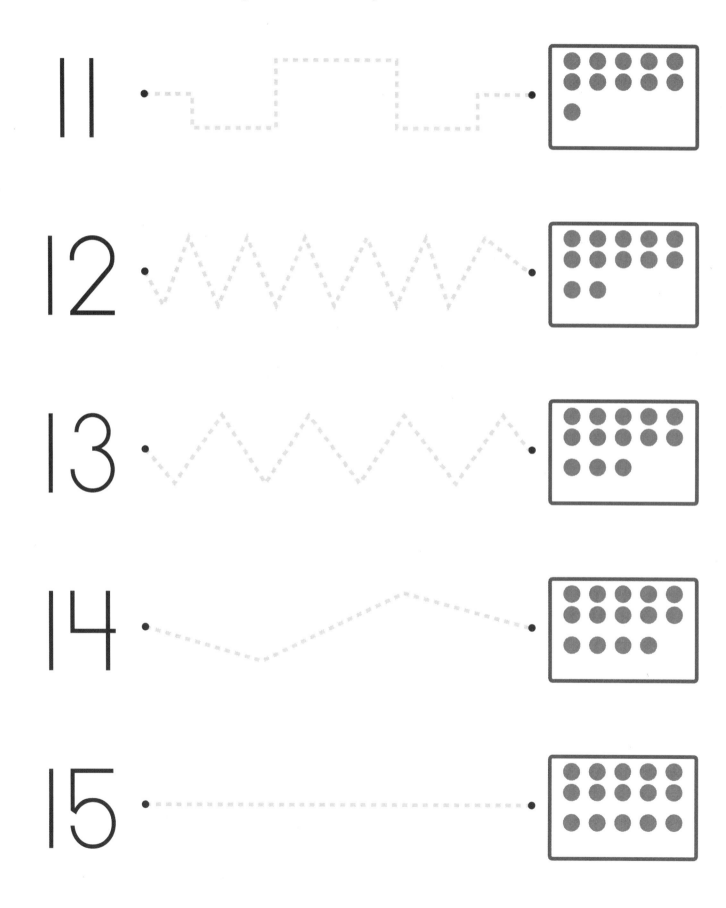

16

17

18

19

20

Tracing Line Practice

Trace each line matching number and picture.

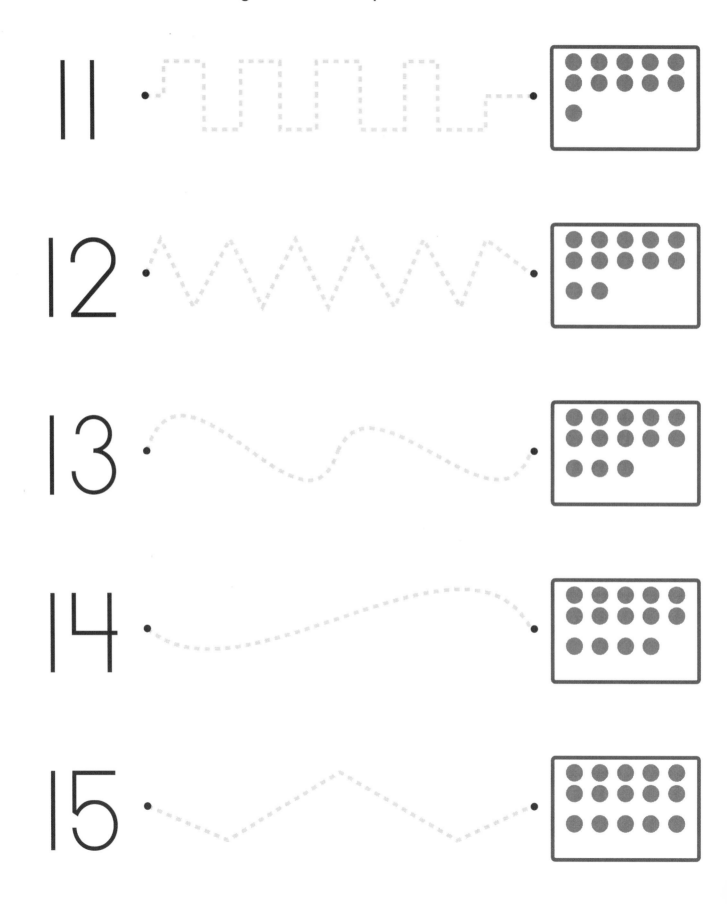

16 •~~~~~~~~~~•

17 •⎍⎍⎍⎍•

18 •∿∿∿∿•

19 •·········•

20 •⎍⎍⎍⎍•

Twenty One

21

21 21 21 21 21

21 21 21 21

21 21 21 21

2 2 2 2

2 2 2 2

2 2 2 2

2 2

2

2

Twenty Two

22

22 22 22 22 22

22 22 22 22 22

22 22 22 22 22

22 22 22 22

22 22 22 22

22 22 22 22

22 22

22

22

Twenty Three

23

23 23 23 23

23 23 23 23

23 23 23 23

23 23 23 23

23 23 23 23

23 23 23 23

23 23

23

23

Twenty Four

24

24 24 24 24 24

24 24 24 24 24

24 24 24 24 24

24 24 24 24 24

24 24 24 24 24

24 24 24 24 24

24 24 24

24

24

Twenty Five

25

25 25 25 25 25

25 25 25 25 25

25 25 25 25 25

25 25 25 25

25 25 25 25

25 25 25 25

25 25

25

25

Twenty Six

26

26 26 26 26 26

26 26 26 26

26 26 26 26

26 26 26 26

26 26 26 26

26 26 26 26

26 26

26

26

Twenty Seven

27

27 27 27 27 27

27 27 27 27 27

27 27 27 27 27

27 27 27 27

27 27 27 27

27 27 27 27

27 27

27

27

Twenty Eight

28

28 28 28 28 28

28 28 28 28 28

28 28 28 28 28

28 28 28 28

28 28 28 28

28 28 28 28

28 28

28

28

Twenty Nine

29

29 29 29 29 29

29 29 29 29 29

29 29 29 29 29

29 29 29 29

29 29 29 29

29 29 29 29

29 29

29

29

Thirty

30

30   30   30   30

30   30   30   30

30   30   30   30

30 30 30 30

30 30 30 30

30 30 30 30

30 30

30

30

Tracing the numbers.

Tracing the numbers.

Tracing the numbers.

Tracing the numbers.

Tracing Line Practice

Trace each line matching number and number word.

21 • · · · · · · · · • Twenty One

22 • · · · · · · · · • Twenty Two

23 • · · · · · · · · • Twenty Three

24 • · · · · · · · · • Twenty Four

25 • · · · · · · · · • Twenty Five

26   Twenty Six

27   Twenty Seven

28   Twenty Eight

29   Twenty Nine

30   Thirty

Tracing Line Practice

Trace each line matching number and number word.

21   •   Twenty One

22   •   Twenty Two

23   •   Twenty Three

24   •   Twenty Four

25   •   Twenty Five

26   Twenty Six

27   Twenty Seven

28   Twenty Eight

29   Twenty Nine

30   Thirty

Tracing Line Practice

Trace each line matching number and number word.

21   Twenty One

22   Twenty Two

23   Twenty Three

24   Twenty Four

25   Twenty Five

26   •·····•   Twenty Six

27   •·····•   Twenty Seven

28   •·····•   Twenty Eight

29   •·····•   Twenty Nine

30   •·····•   Thirty

Tracing Line Practice

Trace each line matching number and picture.

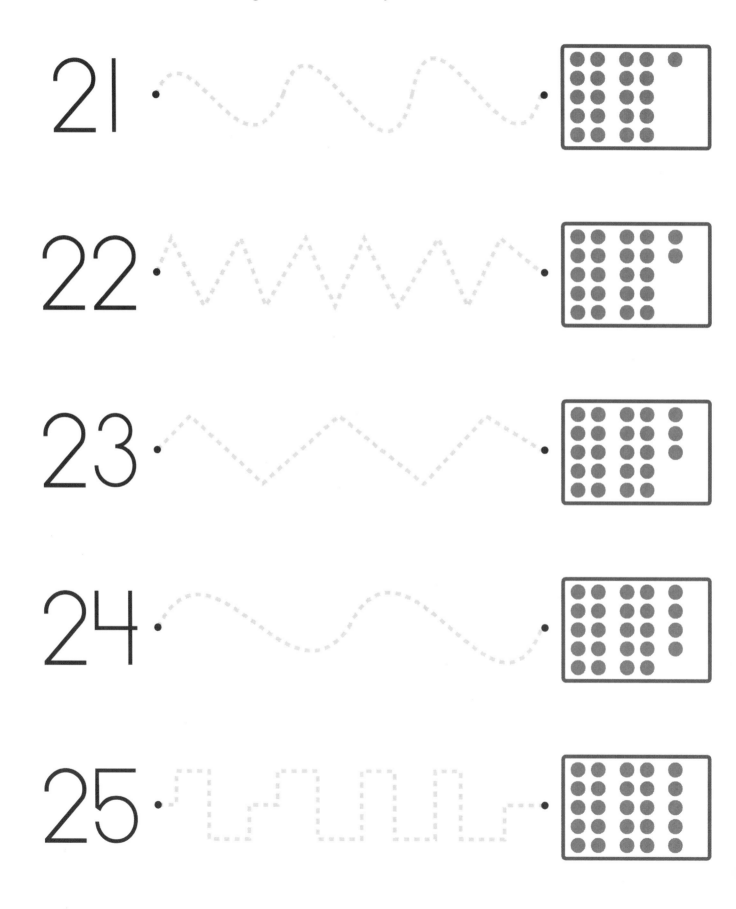

26

27

28

29

30

Tracing Line Practice

Trace each line matching number and picture.

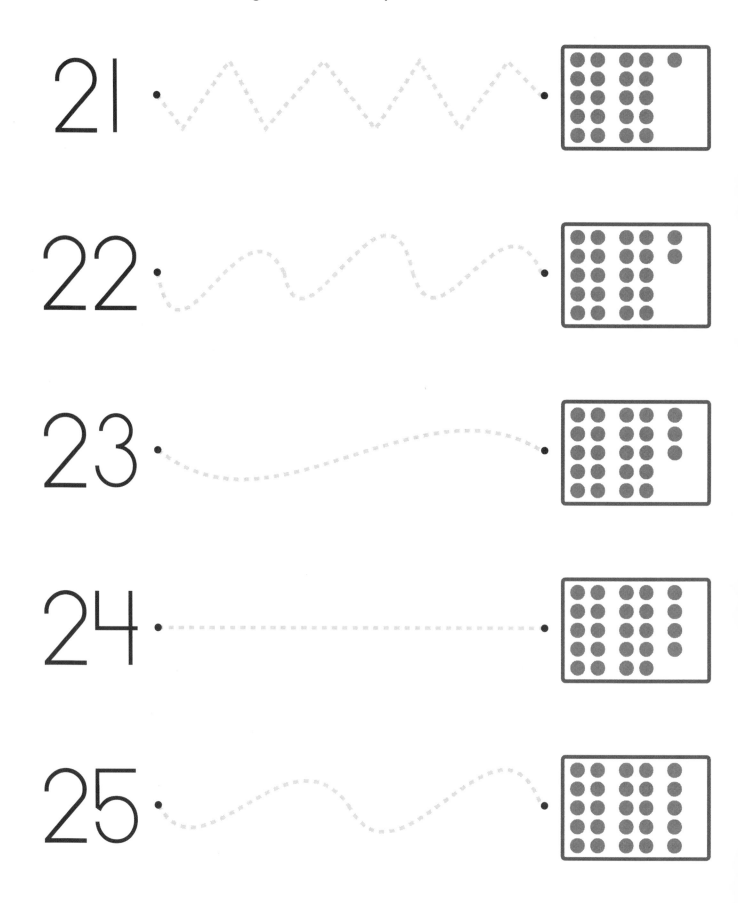

26 •⸱⸱⸱⸱⸱⸱⸱⸱⸱⸱⸱⸱⸱⸱⸱⸱•

27 •⸱⸱⸱⸱⸱⸱⸱⸱⸱⸱⸱⸱⸱⸱⸱⸱•

28 •⸱⸱⸱⸱⸱⸱⸱⸱⸱⸱⸱⸱⸱⸱⸱⸱•

29 •⸱⸱⸱⸱⸱⸱⸱⸱⸱⸱⸱⸱⸱⸱⸱⸱•

30 •⸱⸱⸱⸱⸱⸱⸱⸱⸱⸱⸱⸱⸱⸱⸱⸱•